IRIS and her PRONOUNS

Pronouns for Grades K-2

LILLIE OYEBANJO

Illustrated by:
Ayin Visitacion

To order additional copies of this book, contact:
Xlibris
844-714-8691
www.Xlibris.com
Orders@Xlibris.com

ISBN: 978-1-6641-6761-2 (sc)
ISBN: 978-1-6641-6760-5 (e)

Library of Congress Control Number: 2021907210

Print information available on the last page

Rev. date: 04/30/2021

IRIS AND HER PRONOUNS

(Pronouns for Grades K-2)

To: Teachers and Parents,
This little book can be used as a read aloud text or as a supplemental instructional tool to teach kids about personal pronouns. The punctuation used, or lack thereof, is designed to create a rhythmic effect. It is in "kid speak" talk and a little girl named Iris is teaching her friends how to use personal pronouns.

Personal Pronouns

I, me, my, mine
He, him, his
She her, hers
They, them, their
We, us, our, ours
You, your, yours

I me my mine

I	Hi, I am Iris. I am a girl.
I I I	Iris, Iris, Iris.
	I love ice cream. I I

Me?   Thanks. Is that for me?
Me   me me me.
Me   yes yes yes.
I I I and me me me.

My   This is my ice cream.

My   My my my ice cream.

I I I   Me me me, My my my.

Mine Mine   The ice cream is mine.
Mine mine mine.
I I I   me me me.
My my my, mine mine mine.
All for me.

He him his

Hey Iris. I am Bill. What about me? I love ice cream too.
Bill, Bill, Bill
He he he   He loves ice cream too.
He   He is for a boy.
                Bill, Bill, Bill
He he he   Bill is he he he.

Him
Him him him

Ice cream for him.
He and him are for Bill.

His

His his his

His ice cream, Bill's ice cream.

His his his, His is for Bill.

He he he, him him him.
He he he, him him him.
His his his, his his his.
He and him, him and his.
All for Bill, Bill, Bill, Bill.
One boy, Bill, Bill, Bill.

She her hers

I see Sue. Sue is a girl.
She is for a girl.
Sue, Sue, Sue.
She she she.
Sue is she she she.

Her ice cream. Ice cream for her.
Her her her. She and her are for Sue.
Her ice cream, Sue's ice cream.

The ice cream is hers.
She and her, her and hers.
All for Sue, Sue Sue Sue.
One girl, Sue, Sue, Sue.

We us our ours

We   Look, look. We have ice cream.
          We we we, we we.
We we we, more than one.
We is for more than one.

Us us us   More than one.
Ice cream for us, us, us.
We we we, us us us.   We and us for more than one.
More than one INCLUDING me.
Iris, Bill, and Sue.

Our our, our ice cream. Ice cream for three.
We, us, our, and ours. All for more than one.
We, us, our, and ours. All for Iris, Sue, and Bill.

They, them, their

Iris said to Sue, and Bill.
I see the twins, Mia and Tia.

They have ice cream too.
They they they, they they they.
They is for more than one.
More than one, but NOT me too.
They is for more than one.
They they they, Mia and Tia.

Look at them, Mia and Tia.
Them is for more than one.
They and them, Mia and Tia.
They and them for Mia and Tia.

Their mom is calling them.
Them, Them, them.
Them and their, they and them,
All for Mia and Tia.

You you you
You have ice cream, and
you too.
You is for one.
You is for two.
You you you.

Bill is you.
Sue is you.

Bill and Sue together are you.
You you you.

You is also for more than two.
You can be one.
You can be two.
You can be.
For more than two.
You can be Bill.
You can be Bill and Sue.
And you can be Bill, Sue, Mia, and Tia.
You you you.

your, your, your
Your ice cream, your ice cream.
The ice cream is yours, yours, and yours.
The ice cream is yours, Bill and Sue.
The ice cream is yours, Mia and Tia.
Your ice cream, your ice cream.
Yours and yours for one.
Yours and yours for more than one.

YOUR ice cream, your ice cream.
BUT...Your ice cream is melting.

REVIEW PAGE

I FOR ONE	THEM FOR TWO
I FOR IRIS	AND MORE THAN TWO
ME FOR ONE	THEM FOR NEVER ME
ME FOR IRIS	THEM FOR MIA AND TIA
MY FOR ONE	THEIR FOR TWO
MY FOR IRIS	AND MORE THAN TWO
MINE FOR ONE	THEIR FOR MIA AND TIA
MINE FOR IRIS	THEIR FOR NEVER ME
HE FOR BOY	WE FOR ME AND BILL AND SUE
HE FOR BILL	WE FOR MORE THAN ONE
HIM FOR BOY	US FOR ME AND BILL AND SUE
HIM FOR BILL	US FOR MORE THAN ONE
HIS FOR BOY	OUR FOR ME AND BILL AND SUE
HIS FOR BILL	OUR FOR MORE THAN ONE
SHE FOR ONE	YOU FOR ONE
SHE FOR SUE	YOU FOR TWO
HER FOR ONE	YOU FOR MORE THAN TWO
HER FOR SUE	YOU FOR BILL
THEY FOR TWO	YOU FOR BILL AND SUE
AND MORE THAN TWO	YOU FOR BILL,, SUE, MIA, AND TIA
THEY FOR NEVER ME	BUT YOU FOR NEVER ME
THEY FOR MIA AND TIA	

Printed in the United States
by Baker & Taylor Publisher Services